D1061811

MEGALODON AND OTHER

PREHISTORIC SHARKS

BY TAMMY GAGNE

CAPSTONE PRESS
a capstone imprint

Capstone Captivate is published by Capstone Press, an imprint of Capstone.
1710 Roe Crest Drive, North Mankato, Minnesota 56003
www.capstonepub.com

Copyright © 2022 by Capstone. All rights reserved. No part of this publication may be reproduced in whole or in part, or stored in a retrieval system, or transmitted in any form or by any means, electronic, mechanical, photocopying, recording, or otherwise, without written permission of the publisher.

Library of Congress Cataloging-in-Publication Data
Names: Gagne, Tammy, author.
Title: Megalodon and other prehistoric sharks / by Tammy Gagne.
Description: North Mankato, Minnesota : Capstone Press, 2022. |
Series: Sharks close-up | Includes bibliographical references and index. |
Audience: Ages 8-11 | Audience: Grades 4-6 | Summary: "Great white, bull, and tiger sharks are some of today's most talked-about sharks. But have you met the sharks of yesterday? Each prehistoric shark had its own amazing—and sometimes strange—features. The scissor-tooth shark had teeth in a spiral shape. The giant megalodon was about three times the size of a great white. One small prehistoric shark had a big dorsal fin in the shape of an ironing board! Readers will gobble up all the facts about these early ocean hunters and learn how they compare to modern sharks"-- Provided by publisher.
Identifiers: LCCN 2021004158 (print) | LCCN 2021004159 (ebook) | ISBN 9781663906397 (hardcover) | ISBN 9781663906366 (pdf) | ISBN 9781663906380 (kindle edition)
Subjects: LCSH: Carcharocles megalodon--Juvenile literature.
Classification: LCC QL89.2.C37 G34 2022 (print) | LCC QL89.2.C37 (ebook) | DDC 597.3/3--dc23
LC record available at https://lccn.loc.gov/2021004158
LC ebook record available at https://lccn.loc.gov/2021004159

Editorial Credits
Editor: Carrie Sheely; Designer: Dina Her; Media Researcher: Kelly Garvin; Production Specialist: Tori Abraham

Image Credits
Alamy/Marty Snyderman/Stephen Frink Collection, 20; BluePlanetArchive.com/Makoto Hirose/e-Photo, 27; Capstone Press/Jon Hughes, 9; Newscom: De Agostini Picture Library Universal Images Group, 5, Stephen J. Krasemann/NHPA/Photoshot, 6; Science Source: Christian Darkin, cover, Corey Ford/Stocktrek Images, 21, Gwen Shockey, 18, Jaime Chirinos, 11, 12, 14, 23, 24, JAMES KUETHER, 26, Jeffrey Rotman, 8; Shutterstock: Cq photo juy, 1, frantisekhojdsz, 29, wildestanimal, 28; Wikimedia/Danielle Dufault/PLOS Journals, 17

All internet sites appearing in back matter were available and accurate when this book was sent to press.

TABLE OF CONTENTS

Words in **bold** are in the glossary.

CHAPTER 1

An Amazing Discovery

Imagine finding remains of one of the most powerful creatures that ever lived! In 1867, a man named Jay Terrell did just that. He and his son were visiting the shores of Lake Erie in Ohio. While there, Terrell discovered a **fossil** of what he called a "terrible fish." The fossil was from a kind of **prehistoric** shark. The shark was named *Dunkleosteus terrelli* partly after Terrell. It was one of the fiercest prehistoric sharks.

Long ago, the middle of North America was covered by water. *Dunkleosteus terrelli* swam through this shallow sea. This shark lived about 360 million years ago. It grew up to 20 feet (6.1 meters) long and weighed more than 1 ton. It was about the same size as a modern great white shark.

Dunkleosteus terrelli was a fierce hunter
of the seas in prehistoric times.

FACT

Scientists think there have been only two animals with stronger
jaws than *Dunkleosteus terrelli*. These are the alligator and the
Tyrannosaurus rex dinosaur.

A skull model of *Dunkleosteus terrelli*

People who visit the Cleveland Museum of Natural History can see the fossil of a *Dunkleosteus terrelli* skull. It includes two sets of fang-like teeth and sturdy jaws. This shark used its sharp teeth and strong jaws to hunt other fish.

Dunkleosteus terrelli died out millions of years ago. But modern sharks are related to this shark and other prehistoric sharks. Modern sharks **evolved** over time. They share many features with their prehistoric relatives, such as fins and sharp teeth. But some sharks that lived millions of years ago had very different features. A few looked downright odd!

FACT

Sharks are among the oldest animals on the planet. They lived long before dinosaurs, insects, or even trees!

CHAPTER 2

The Biggest Prehistoric Sharks

Movies about sharks often focus on the biggest and fiercest modern **species,** such as great whites. If movies would have existed in prehistoric times, other giant sharks would have been the stars!

The tooth of a great white shark (left) and the tooth of a megalodon (right)

Megalodon's strong jaws and sharp teeth helped make it a skilled hunter.

Megalodon

Megalodons were the largest sharks that ever lived. Most megalodons measured about 50 feet (15 m) long. But scientists think that some reached 82 feet (25 m) long! The biggest megalodons could have weighed up to 70 tons. That's the weight of about 10 male African elephants. The biggest modern hunting sharks are great whites. They can reach 21 feet (6.4 m) long.

Megalodons died out about 2.6 million years ago. Scientists are not sure why. Some think it was because of climate change. This could have caused the **prey** of megalodons to die out. Megalodons needed a lot of food to survive. They ate the largest seals and turtles in the ocean. Scientists think that eventually the animals did not have enough to eat.

Scientists also think climate change could have made the water temperatures cooler. They think megalodons had to maintain a high body temperature. They would have had to stay in warmer waters to hunt and raise their young. Some prey, such as whales, could have moved to the cooler waters easily. But megalodons wouldn't have been able to move to cooler waters.

A megalodon attacks a whale.

Modern Whale Migration and Megalodons

Megalodons may be the reason whales **migrate** today. Modern whales such as humpback whales move to cooler waters seasonally. Whales could have begun doing this to get away from megalodons. Whales were likely main prey of megalodons. People have found whale fossils with megalodon teeth stuck in them.

Scientists believe the Ginsu shark's tail helped it reach fast speeds to catch prey.

FACT

The Ginsu shark was named after a popular knife because of its teeth. The Ginsu knife is known for being especially sharp.

Ginsu Shark

Ginsu sharks lived about 100 million years ago. They were the largest sharks of their time. They measured up to 23 feet (7 m) long. These sharks had hundreds of razor-sharp teeth. Their teeth helped the sharks become fierce **predators**. Ginsu sharks made meals of fish that were bigger than they were. These sharks also ate the largest sea turtles that ever lived, *Archelon ischyros*. The turtles grew to about 12 feet (3.7 m) long.

Ptychodus

Sharks in a group called *Ptychodus* lived more than 85 million years ago. These sharks grew to about 33 feet (10 m) long. They had many flat teeth. Scientists think these sharks may have had up to 1,000 teeth in their jaws! Their flat teeth would have helped them crush shellfish. Experts think these sharks mainly lived near the seafloor.

A scissor-tooth shark swims
near a large school of fish.

Scissor-tooth Shark

Scissor-tooth sharks lived about 300 million years ago. They measured about 20 feet (6.1 m) long. This is about the size of modern great whites. But the mouths of scissor-tooth sharks looked completely different than those of great whites. These sharks had two curved arcs of teeth. Each one pointed outward.

Scissor-tooth sharks also hunted differently from other sharks. Most sharks kill prey by biting. But scientists think scissor-tooth sharks thrashed their heads up and down instead. This movement created slashing wounds on the other animals. Sometimes it would slice prey in half.

CHAPTER 3

Small Prehistoric Sharks

Many modern sharks are small. One kind is smaller than your hand! Many prehistoric sharks were small too. These smaller sharks had some things in common with their larger relatives. But they often differed from them in more ways than just size.

Spiny Shark

Spiny sharks lived about 360 million years ago. These fish had skeletons made of cartilage. Modern sharks also have skeletons made from this material. Cartilage is softer than bone. Spiny sharks were named for the spiny pieces of cartilage that helped support their fins.

Spiny sharks had large eyes at the front of their heads.

Spiny sharks in the *Climatius* group had two fins on the top of their backs and several fins underneath their bodies.

Spiny sharks rarely grew to more than 12 inches (31 centimeters) in length. They didn't look or behave like miniature versions of today's sharks. They had small heads and long bodies. They looked far less fierce. Spiny sharks had large eyes and short snouts. They used sight far more than their sense of smell.

Spiny sharks were filter feeders. This meant they trapped tiny food particles from the water with their gills. Pieces of cartilage in the gills helped make this process work. Although spiny sharks were small, they were the largest filter feeders alive at the time.

Pristiophorus Striatus

Being small didn't stop some prehistoric sharks from being great hunters. *Pristiophorus striatus* lived between 5 and 23 million years ago. It was about 3.5 feet (1.1 m) long. It had an extra-long snout lined with sharp teeth to tear prey. Other types of sharks with these features still exist today. Scientists call them saw sharks.

Modern saw sharks such as longnose saw sharks have long snouts like their prehistoric relatives did.

A group of *Xenacanthus* sharks

Xenacanthus

Sharks in the group *Xenacanthus* lived about 360 million years ago. Sometimes they are called eel sharks because they looked like the snake-like eels found in modern oceans. The sharks had small heads and long, narrow bodies like today's eels. They measured about 3.2 feet (1 m) long.

Unlike other sharks, *Xenacanthus* had a long, ribbon-like fin that ran the length of its body. It also had a sharp spine on the back of its skull. The shark likely used this body part for protection.

FACT

Like other sharks, *Xenacanthus*'s skeleton was made of cartilage. But the spine on its skull was made of bone. Scientists think the spine was **venomous**. The venom would have harmed predators.

21

CHAPTER 4

Sharks with Unusual Features

Each prehistoric shark was unique. But some had especially unusual features. If you would have seen these sharks, you probably would have done a double take!

Scaleless Shark

The scaleless shark swam through Earth's waters 380 million years ago. It didn't have a fierce appearance. It had a small head and a thin body. It measured about 4 feet (1.2 m) long. It was also much less muscular than many other sharks at the time.

The scaleless shark was named for its most obvious feature. Unlike most other sharks, it had no **scales**. Its thin skin made it harder for the scaleless shark to defend itself. But having no scales also made the animal much lighter and faster. It used its speed to catch prey.

Scaleless sharks had long, streamlined bodies to help them swim quickly.

Some scientists think the front dorsal fins on male anvil sharks might have been used to attract females.

Anvil Shark

The anvil shark was among the oddest-looking sharks. It lived more than 300 million years ago.

The male anvil shark had a dorsal fin on its back that was flat on top. The anvil shark was named after the iron block that this dorsal fin looked like. The fin was covered in **denticles**. Modern sharks still have these small, toothlike scales all over their skin. The top of the anvil shark's head also had denticles.

Bandringa

Sharks in the group *Bandringa* lived about 310 million years ago. Their standout feature was a long, spoonbill-shaped snout. Adults grew to about 10 feet (3 m) long. Their snouts stretched up to half their body length. The sharks might have used these snouts to dig out buried prey at the seafloor.

Buzzsaw Shark

The buzzsaw shark wasn't actually a shark. But it was a relative of modern sharks. Also called *Helicoprion*, this fish lived about 290 million years ago. It was named for its unusual tooth pattern. The fish's teeth were arranged in a spiral pattern. This made its mouth look like the blade of a circular saw. The appearance was so odd that it took scientists a long time to figure out what its fossils actually were. At first, many thought they were looking at ancient seashells.

Helicoprion did not have upper teeth. It relied on its spiral teeth for attacks.

A modern goblin shark swims in the deep sea.

Goblin Shark

Fossils of the goblin shark are much easier to identify. This shark had a long, flat snout that extended forward. It also had a highly unusual jaw. It could come unhinged when the animal ate large prey. The goblin shark is still alive today. It has lived on Earth for 125 million years.

A great white shark swims through the ocean near Guadalupe Island, Mexico.

Understanding Sharks

Studying prehistoric sharks helps people understand modern sharks better. The sharks that swim through today's oceans get many of their traits from their ancient relatives. Large jaws, big dorsal fins, and sharp teeth are common traits of both modern and prehistoric sharks.

Over time, many sharks evolved to better match their environments. Prehistoric hammerhead sharks first lived about 20 million years ago. Today, several hammerhead species still exist. They look a lot like their prehistoric relatives. But scientists think they have better eyesight and sense of smell than the hammerheads of long ago. They use these senses for finding food.

Each shark has evolved in its own interesting way. We can't go back to see the sharks that swam the seas millions of years ago. But if you could, which one would you want to see?

A great hammerhead shark hunts for food.

Glossary

cartilage (KAHR-tuh-lij)—the strong, bendable material that forms some body parts of people and animals

denticle (DEN-ti-kuhl)—a small, toothlike scale that covers a shark's skin

evolve (i-VAHLV)—to change gradually over time

fossil (FAH-suhl)—the remains or traces of plants and animals that are preserved as rock

migrate (MYE-grate)—to travel from one area to another regularly

predator (PRED-uh-tur)—an animal that hunts other animals for food

prehistoric (pree-hi-STOR-ik)—from a time before history was recorded

prey (PRAY)—an animal hunted by another animal for food

scale (SKALE)—one of the small, hard plates that covers the skin of most fish and reptiles

species (SPEE-sheez)—a group of animals with similar features

venomous (VEN-uhm-us)—able to produce a poison called venom

Read More

Rake, Matthew. *Prehistoric Sea Beasts*. Minneapolis: Hungry Tomato, 2017.

Skerry, Brian, Elizabeth Carney, and Sarah Wassner Flynn. *The Ultimate Book of Sharks: Your Guide to These Fierce and Fantastic Fish*. Washington, D.C.: National Geographic, 2018.

Zoehfeld, Kathleen Weidner. *Prehistoric: Dinosaurs, Megalodons, and Other Fascinating Creatures of the Deep Past*. Tonbridge, Kent, United Kingdom; Greenbelt, MD: What on Earth Books, 2019.

Internet Sites

Active Wild: Megalodon Facts
activewild.com/megalodon-facts/

BBC: Earth: The Epic History of Sharks
bbc.com/earth/story/20151003-the-epic-history-of-sharks

National Geographic Kids: Goblin Shark
kids.nationalgeographic.com/animals/fish/goblin-shark/

Index